Plants Make Their Own Food

by Julie K. Lundgren

Science Content Editor:
Kristi Lew

rourkeeducationalmedia.com

Science content editor: Kristi Lew

A former high school teacher with a background in biochemistry and more than 10 years of experience in cytogenetic laboratories, Kristi Lew specializes in taking complex scientific information and making it fun and interesting for scientists and non-scientists alike. She is the author of more than 20 science books for children and teachers.

www.rourkeeducationalmedia.com

Photo credits: Cover © Jag_cz, Triff, Sam DCruz, ra2 studio, Cover logo frog © Eric Pohl, test tube © Sergey Lazarev; Table Of Contents © Granite; Page 4 © IKO; Page 5 © Jaimie Duplass; Page 7 © Kevin Eaves; Page 9 © shirophoto; Page 10 © Juriah Mosin; Page 11 © Ewa Walicka; Page 12 © Neeila; Page 13 © Alexanderus; Page 14 © Dmitri Melnik; Page 15 © Granite; Page 16 © CREATISTA; Page 17 © Aleksandr Bryliaev; Page 18 © eans; Page 19 © Yossi Manor; Page 20 © Zeljko Radojko; Page 21 © Alexey Antipov

Editor: Kelli Hicks

My Science Library series produced for Rourke by Blue Door Publishing, Florida

Library of Congress Cataloging-in-Publication Data

Lundgren, Julie K.
 Plants make their own food / Julie K. Lundgren.
    p. cm. -- (My science library)
 Includes bibliographical references and index.
 ISBN 978-1-61741-747-4 (Hard cover) (alk. paper)
 ISBN 978-1-61741-949-2 (Soft cover)
 1. Plants--Juvenile literature. 2. Photosynthesis--Juvenile literature. I. Title.
 QK49.L866 2012
 580--dc22
                                        2011004760

Rourke Educational Media
Printed in the United States of America,
North Mankato, Minnesota

rourkeeducationalmedia.com

customerservice@rourkeeducationalmedia.com • PO Box 643328 Vero Beach, Florida 32964

Table of Contents

Plug Into the Sun

The Sun provides Earth with light, a form of **energy**. Light energy from the Sun fuels life on Earth.

The Sun bathes Earth in warmth and light.

Using the Sun's light energy, green plants and a few other life forms, such as kelp, make their own food in a **process** called **photosynthesis**.

Though they are not plants, kelp can perform photosynthesis, too.

Food Factories

Plants use photosynthesis to change two **ingredients** into a simple sugar. The ingredients are water and a gas called carbon dioxide.

Plants use the sugar they make to live and grow.

Roots take in water. Leaves **absorb carbon dioxide** from the air. Sunlight provides the energy for photosynthesis to work.

carbon dioxide

water

11

Chlorophyll absorbs the Sun's light energy. The plant then uses this captured energy to change carbon dioxide and water into sugar.

chlorophyll

Chlorophyll gives plants their green color.

Besides sugar, photosynthesis makes a gas called **oxygen**. Plants make more oxygen than they need, so they let go of the extra oxygen.

Gases enter and exit plant leaves through very tiny openings.

Photosynthesis

oxygen

chlorophyll

carbon
dioxide

water

15

The Air We Breathe

Both animals and plants need air. People need oxygen from air and plants need carbon dioxide.

Animals help plants with photosynthesis by breathing out carbon dioxide.

17

People and animals need to breathe in the oxygen plants release during photosynthesis. And plants need to use the carbon dioxide people and animals breathe out.

oxygen

carbon dioxide

How Animals and Plants Help Each Other

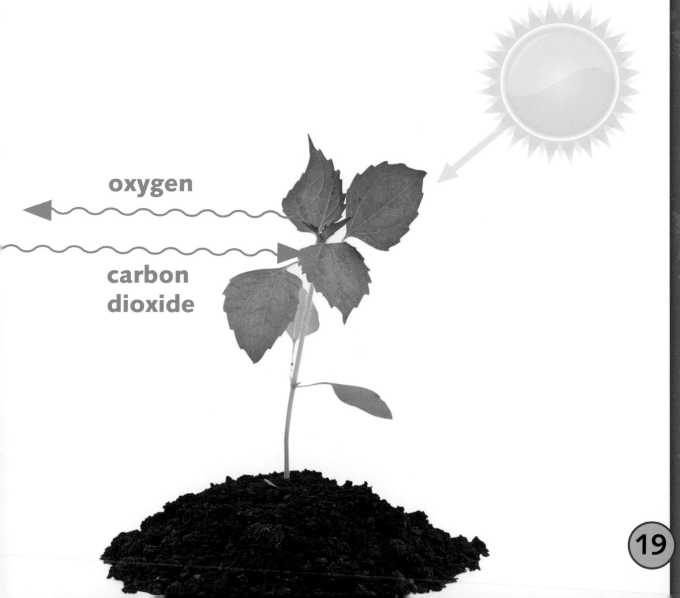

oxygen

carbon
dioxide

Animals and people rely on plants for food. They also need oxygen from plants. Without plants and photosynthesis, animals and people would not survive.

Thank you, plants!

1. What do plants need to make their own food?

2. Why are plants important to life on Earth?

3. How do the gases that animals and plants produce benefit each other?

Glossary

absorb (ab-ZORB): to take in liquid or gas

carbon dioxide (KAR-buhn dye-OK-side): a gas that people and animals breathe out as waste

chlorophyll (KLOR-uh-fill): the stuff in plants that causes the green color and traps light energy from the Sun for photosynthesis

energy (en-ur-jee): the ability to do work or make changes happen

ingredients (in-GREE-dee-uhnts): things that go into a recipe to make something else

oxygen (OK-suh-juhn): a gas that plants make and that people and animals breathe in

photosynthesis (foh-toh-SIN-thuh-siss): the way green plants make their own food

process (PRAH-sess): a series of steps to make or do something

Index

Websites

www.exploringnature.org/db/detail.php?dbID=32&detID=1208

www.ftexploring.com/me/photosyn1.html

www.pbs.org/wgbh/nova/methuselah/phot_flash.html

www.realtrees4kids.org/sixeight/letseat.htm

About the Author

As a child, Julie K. Lundgren lived near Lake Superior where she once grew a giant turnip and had many pets. Her interest in plants and animals led her to a degree in biology. She lives in Minnesota with her family.